Honey & Blooms

Debi Mukherjee

BookLeaf
Publishing

India | USA | UK

Presentation by *BookLeaf Publishing*

Web: www.bookleafpub.com

E-mail: info@bookleafpub.com

ISBN: 9789360943349

First edition 2024

*"To all the extraordinary women who have
inspired the verses,*

To my little boy, and the love of my life,

And last by certainly not the least,

*To you, dear reader, for breathing life into these
pages."*

ACKNOWLEDGEMENT

I will forever be thankful to Dadan,

for storing my notebooks containing the poems I attempted to compose as a child.

To my partner,

for cheering me on to write again.

PREFACE

Dear Reader,

Come, Do take my hands,
Embark with me to uncharted lands!
In verses spun with love so rare,
We'll journey through our emotions with care.

This book of poetry, is a trove,
Of women's lives, of dreams and love.
From tender youth to wiser age,
Each page unfolds a heartfelt stage.

With every line, a story told,
Of struggles faced as dreams unfold.
In joy and sorrow, love and pain,
The essence of womanhood we'll gain.

Thank you for joining me, dear reader,
On this journey,
Together, let's explore,
The beauty of life's poetry.

Resting

Shut-eye, dear girl, what is that?
I have mountains to climb,
And villages to put to sleep.
So can I afford to take a nap?

Resting, dear girl, maybe when I'm older
Now the world awaits,
I have finally made it this far,
The doors they have opened.

The dreams our mothers had, they have to be
realised,
Look how far ahead men have reached, I hear
the war cry from women—
Let's leave no stones unturned
To prove to this world our worth.
So when do I rest, my girl?

The Girl

Mother I see you toiling all day
When do we have time to play?
We are here now, do not think of tomorrow.

What is on your mind?
I urge you, our thoughts entwine;
Look Mother, there is no war
No one cries out to do it all.
There is no dream that you haven't fulfilled,
In your love, are my fears stilled.

Mother, we have reached for the sky,
With courage that dared to soar and fly,
Our spirit sang, unfettered and spry,
Through valleys deep and peaks so high.

All I ask of you is this,
Amidst this chaos, to find your bliss,
Embrace me with a gentle kiss
Let go of worries, this dull abyss.
A woman is everything already, we know this.

Modernity

She walks with grace, her tales untold,
Her kohl-lined eyes, a beauty to behold,
She navigates worlds, new and old,
And strives for each day, patient and bold.

Beyond the confines of cultural norms,
She holds her own, weathering storms,
In her spirit, a fire burns bright,
She is the modern woman, embodying her might.

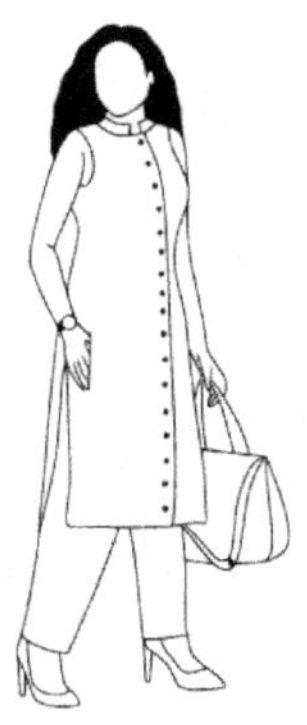

The Girl under a Table

In the glow of a memory, I have of that day,
Underneath a table, she was hiding away.
Mini-bangs veiling her forehead's close,
Thick-rimmed glasses perched on her nose.

She was dressed in a white frock, and was
pouring over a book;
When they called out to her, she barely looked.
The sun rays brimmed over her shoulders in a
dance,
She was immersed in her book in a perfect
trance.

I bent underneath and crawled towards her,
With a child's curiosity I drew nearer;
"Anne of Green Gables," she said, was her
favourite book,
She asked me to join her, and take a closer look.

Delighted to join into the realm of words, we set
sail;
Thus began our friendship, a cherished tale.

Red is within Her

In the mirror's gaze, she met her reflection,
A woman now.
She has Red on her.

Relinquishing the body of a child and poised for
the new,
She strides with pride,
Facing this natural tide, she thinks not to hide.
Red is within her.

Nani and the Night Jasmine

"Come along, my dear," Nani said with care,
"Watch your step, it's slippery out there."
I clutched the flower basket tight,
As Nani helped me stay upright.

She pulled down the branches, one by one,
To collect the blooms, oh what fun!
Hibiscus red, Magnolia white,
Marigold golden, such a delight!
My favourite was the 'Shiuli phool'—Night
jasmine so divine,
It's elegance with my memories, forever
entwined.

My Nani, your love, like its fragrance, lingers
here too,
A memory I treasure, and love going back to.
Our folklore says, 'Shiuli' she bestows love and
healing,
I find this memory of you, my Nani, forever
besotting.

Baby Sister

The very first day when I held her,
She had batted her large eyes and grabbed my
finger,
I almost felt a start, like a connection had
sparked, in our hearts—
I think she felt it too.

In our first gaze, magic's seed was sown,
A bond forever to cherish, and to own.
Through joys and sorrows, and everything else
in between,
Our souls remain entwined.

Caged

She married her love, her dreams aglow,
Fulfilled at last, like tales she knew
Her world rejoiced at their nuptials, in love's
bright hue,
A celebration of union, a dream come true.

Yet with time she felt, her reality strayed,
Her rosy path, now dimmed and frayed.
What she had dreamt, was far from sight,
Her lover's gaze, no longer bright.

He who once listened, tyrannised her in ways,
No time for her, no words he says.
Rules, expectations from her were tall,
To serve, to obey, at Society's call.

Familiar roles in her home, she'd seen before,
T'was different this time, her turn to take on
more
Relinquishing her autonomy, her own dreams
torn,
She felt trapped, her spirit sore.

In her despair, she lamented.
But what stopped her from moving ahead ?
Was it Love, Wealth or Society then,
That raised a woman to lower her head?

Ode to Sensuality

She moves gently like a breeze,
Softly she passes by, such a tease,

Her eyes they smoulder, in a sensual haze,
She enthrals them with a craving gaze.

An enchantress, she casts out their deepest
gloom,
Her skin, an ode to honey and bloom.

She smiles at them like a Queen, a seductress's
art,
They go back for more, with bewitched hearts.

Brown Girl

The Sun has kissed your skin at birth,
And made you one of them—
The sand, the sea and mountains, you see,
They pay homage to your beauty!

Brown—the colour of earth itself!
Girl, you are a wonder, no one told you about.

Holding the Sun in your smile,
You embrace the ocean, like a child.
And the sand in your hair, they shine so wild!
They are spellbound by your beauty!

Dark, like the woods so deep,
Girl, you are a wonder, no one told you about.

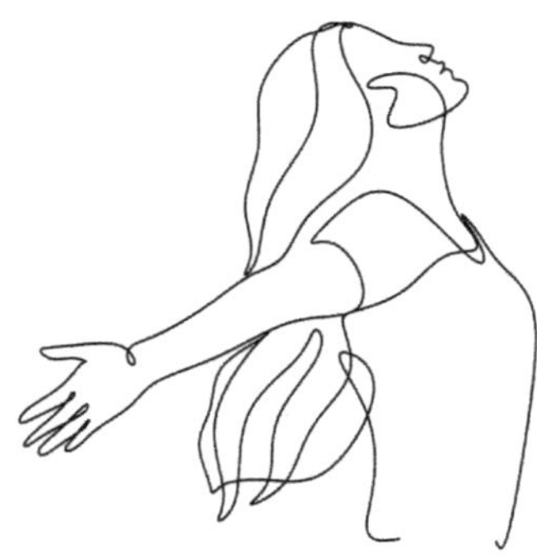

Exalted love

She quietly held her baby in her womb,
And smiled, although uncertainty loomed.
Her dream was coming true, yet she was unsure,
Unable to fathom a future, she felt nothing more.

The flush of mornings filled her with dread,
To bring a child into this world, she wasn't
prepared.
Then the day arrived, when her labour pains
abated,
Finally, in her arms, her newborn waited.

Her little one, once part of her core,
Now cried out, and her heart felt sore.
A love beyond words, beyond compare,
A bond so deep, it stripped her bare.

A love that can put words to shame,
A love that can make the sky cry out, there's no
compare—an exalted love.
She felt a delusional joy, just to watch him,
He grabbed at her finger and made her smile, as
if almost teasing—"Was it worth it, all the
waiting, and the dreams?"

City Girl

A City that never sleeps, they say, where life's a
whirl,
A melting pot of cultures, great vitality unfurls,
So hardworking, yet not flashy,
In her I see my identity—a City girl.

The sky-scrappers, and the serene sea, I adore
her vibe,
Always ready for something new, never
subscribing to a tribe.
I am up at dawn, while I ponder all
this—admiring her skyline,
Sipping my first cup of tea,
While I take a minute to soak this in—she's the
Maximum city.

She's given me friends, opportunities, memories
so grand,

From high school days and into the workforce,
holding my hand
Then I turn to the wall clock, time to rush to the
beat,
Out into the day, with hustle and heat.
So I scurry out to complete my morning routine,
When evening comes, there's a party to greet.

Where friends will gather, 'neath the City's glow,
How wonderful to be young, and free to grow.
Living life where I want to be,
In the heart of the City, wild and free.

Companion

She disliked the same clamour of late-night
affairs,
Heady pub crawls and strangers' stares.
She had no desire to mingle everyday with new
faces,
And receive compliments, she wanted to spare.

Then one day, she met her, a friend
Who really could get her,
Who delved beyond the surface,
And went right into her mind's window,
She cut out all the circus.

Hours flew by in their deep conversation's spree,
Time was racing fast, yet her heart felt free.
At first, she held back, kept thoughts to herself,
Too bold, too strange, too outlandish she felt
to share with someone else.

At first she brought up her thoughts subtly, as if
a dance,
But met with a smile or a glint in her eyes,
Sometimes a merry hyena-like laugh, her marks
of approval,
She had come to like her many ways, and was
fulfilled.

In this understanding, she found her world anew,
A companion, a confidante, so true.

Unborn Girl Child

In my dreams, dear girl, you had graced me with
your light,
A vision my darling Ishani, in the depths of the
night,
As the Goddess incarnate, you shone so bright.

We worship everyday, the Goddess herself
On marble pedestals, adorned with care,
With garlands of flowers, we offer our prayers.
As the Desecrator of troubles, we hold her dear.

Yet, we dare not bear you, Ishani my dear,
Unfounded beliefs, our hearts filled with fear.

Being Fearless

She pedalled uphill, the air crisp and cold,
Ventured deep in the woods, her spirit bold,
At last she approached a lodging, aged and
forlorn.

Her Mother's caution echoed, yet she was drawn.
Ignoring the warnings, she circled 'round,
Slightly hesitant of the unknown, unbound.

But as she strolled, she found a mansion so old,
And to its rear, a beauty to behold!
A river flowed, its waters so cold,
She dipped her hand, felt the tranquil flow.
She played with the water and gave it a quiver,
And saw her face smiling back at her.

Returning home, her heart light and free,

She vowed to escort Mother to see,
Hoping that she would also keep,
An open mind, embracing new dreams.

Tribute to 'Peethe'

'Peethe' is a poetry by itself,
For those unaware, it is a love language,
Crafted by mothers with care,
For families—a tradition, as a New Year's fare.

Delicately formed in loving maternal hands; for
generations so old,
With every bite, it transforms into stories told.
The luscious coconut and palm jaggery hidden
In the aromatic folds of the rice flour crepes
within—
'Peethe' is a dessert that is a sensory delight.
But the anticipation of the food is beguiling too!
Through the corridors, does the aroma waft,
Igniting memories, warm and soft.
To a Bengali, 'Peethe' is more than a treat,
It's nostalgia, love, a memory sweet.

And as the flavours dissolve upon the tongue,
It resembles a poem, beautifully strung.

My Treasure trove

In the narrow by-lanes of Jodhpur's ancient
streets,
I stumbled upon a treasure trunk, replete.
Adorned with intricate artwork and mirrors, it
gleamed,
Centuries old, an ornate trunk it seemed.

Initially a souvenir that caught my eye, soon
became my vessel, by my side.
A repository of connections, where my
memories reside.
With time, it travelled with me to each city
where I moved,
Holding in it my recollections, my treasure
trove.

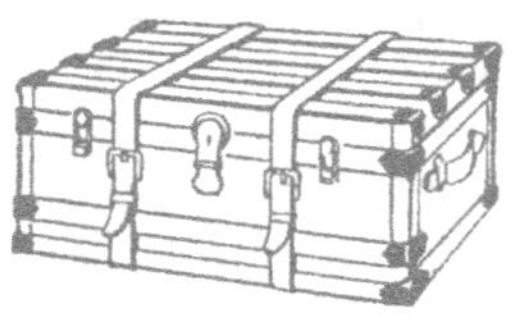

On a quiet evening, as the sun bid adieu,
I delved into its depths, my memories to review,
And out they tumbled, in waves,
Little notes, faded photos, tokens from the past,

Each item—a treasure, a memory to last.
Entry tickets to tissue napkins, each holds a tale,
A trinket or two, and notes to self, without fail.
My trunk, a whirlpool of memories, it holds
within,
A life well-lived, a journey akin.

As I grow older, I hold the chest close,
To relive the memories and the treasure it holds,
T'is worth more to me than a potful of gold.
A silent witness to the tales new and old.

A lost Love

Thirty winters have passed since I met her,
Yet in my mind, her face remains clear.

She was a free spirit, and everything I yearned to
be,
We were always together, two a company.
As young girls we had shared our fantasies, our
dreams and tears,
Then ventured into the unknown together,
conquering our fears.

But one fateful day, she had to depart,
I bade her adieu with a heaving heart.
With moist eyes, we bid our goodbyes,
As she spread her wings, to new skies.

In her presence, my spirit soared,
She might have been the friend I loved.

Midsummer Reverie

As a teenager, I recall midsummer days,
I'd emerge from my reveries to find my mother
working on something at her own pace.
I'd walk in on her, peeling an orange or poaching
an egg in the kitchen;
And when she noticed me, she'd ask for a
helping hand.
Sometimes she'd hum a lovely tune,
While watering the plants, or sewing on an
intricate piece of embroidery.
I'd often marvel at her, at the finesse of the
craftsmanship, of the way she sang or how
delicious her meals would always taste.
She'd sit me down and share a funny story or
two from her youth,
As we sipped on hot ginger flavoured milk tea,
while dipping Marie biscuits in them till they
were softened,
Only our favourite way to have them!
Those stretched out lazy summer days feel like a
dream.

A *Femme fatale's* Tale

Her smile and a wink, enthralled by her spell,
A Femme fatale, with tales to tell.
Her touch seductive, burning down the spine,
Tangled in her web she will have you confined.

Yet, old wife's tales tells a story untold,
Of a woman who's lost, and a heart grown cold.
She seeked solace in her lover from the past,
Their flames flickered out, didn't mean to last.

She dances now in shadows, seeking fleeting
delight,
A femme fatale, in the depths of the night.
Beneath the facade, there's a longing to flee,
Or someday to own her destiny.

Circle of Life

In the twilight hours, she sits by the fire's glow,
A lifetime etched upon her face, stories of her
own.
Her hands, weathered by time, now rest on her
lap,
They have lines of her life like an intricate map.

She's walked through storms and basked in the
sun,
Raised her children with love, some battles lost
while some won.
In the tapestry of life, she's woven her part,
Facing countless trials, each a brushstroke, as if
life was an art.

She reflects on her grown children with a tender
smile,
Proudly watching as they navigate life's mile.
Independence and strength, values she'd
instilled,
Now on they go, as she watches.

New life blossoms before her;
As she gazes upon the little children's faces,
She sees the future, in their embraces,
A life richly woven, with love indeed,
The circle of life that she has beaded.

Dear Son (Sonnet)

My Dear, as you journey through life,
embracing the unknown,
May you set your spirit free, with the courage
you own.
Loving passionately, yet never overpowering,
may you be,
Receiving inspiration from life itself, so you can
see.

May your cup of experiences always have room
to flow,
And may you encounter loss and victory, aiding
your growth.
Respect other's agency, as you value your own,
In life's tapestry, let compassion be shown.

Lead with courage, when facing the devil's stare,
May Life's lessons dispel away your fears.
Wear your heart on your sleeve or not, or maybe
dance happily in the rain,
The world is yours, with its joy and pain.
May you always find your way, my Dear,
Passion be your compass, helping you steer.

Care

The other day, as we conversed, my son gently
asked, "Mamma, why do you care?"
Thoughts flooded in, as I pondered, and they lay
bare.

"Caring, like a river, runs deep within me,
Moulding me, shaping who I came to be.
To speak with care, ensuring kindness is
received,
To dress with care, so no one feels aggrieved.
Careful not to raise my voice in a heated tone,
As I grew up, these lessons I have known."

But why was I taught to live with such profound
care?
Was it a virtue learned in polite society's snare?
Why the negative connotation with "careless"
then?

If you ask me today, I will say: "It's wise to
choose between them,
To sift the important from the fray,
To be 'careless' in some, not in a heedless way.
Then can we focus on what matters truly, with
intent,
Not for others, but our own contentment.

So, my son, I care because it's who I am,

And I'm learning to be 'careless', whenever I
can."

Longing

It's been many months since our paths have crossed,
Do you still think of it as much as I do?
The way you held my hand that night, I still ache
for that tender caress,
And my body, it craves for your warm embrace,
And the twinkle in your eyes, they would reflect
in mine.
Was it just a passing phase for you?

Without you in my life, I fear I'll have no heart,
Like a wet ball of sand, now dried; I'm falling
apart.
As rain patters on the window sill, I ache for
your touch;
Way you had run your fingers down the nape of
my neck,
Playful and light,
Do you imagine them, still?
Making circles at the bottom of my spine?
Sending shivers in the night,
Oh how cold it feels to imagine holding you,
when you're not really here!

Outside the wind howls to the sky, echoing my plea,
Just as my heart yearns, Can you come back to me?

Darjeeling blues

In the hill station, where the misty peaks meet the sky,

I caught a glimpse of her rosy cheeks, as I walked by

In the serene tea estates of Darjeeling.

As the leaves swayed in the gentle breeze,

Her eyes met mine, in a moment of tease.

In hill's embrace, where dreams take flight,

I found my muse in the soft twilight.

I'd hear her laughter, echoing through the valley,

As I pen these lines, and reminisce.

She lingers on, like a gentle breeze,

A moment when I was enthralled by a beauty
from the hills.

www.ingramcontent.com/pod-product-compliance
Lightning Source LLC
La Vergne TN
LVHW010832200726

843508LV00012B/2574